GO.>

DEDICATION:
TO NATE, KARIN, AND ELISE
MAY THE LIGHT OF JESUS BLAZE IN YOU FOR ALL THE WORLD
TO SEE – FOR YOUR GROWTH, OTHERS' GOOD, AND GOD'S GLORY.

Acknowledgments: Thanks to Teen Missions International and the 1980 Venezuela Team for jolting me awake and aiming me down God's road. Thanks to Paul Bertelson and YouthWorks, along with Seth Barnes and Adventures in Missions for coaxing me to write my original ACTS mission prep curriculum. Thanks to Mark Oestreicher and Youth Specialties for pursuing this book. And thanks to Mindi Conradi for bringing youth missions to Peace Lutheran—and for so capably pulling together trips that alter our youth and their worlds forever.

CONTENTS

TO YOU—THE STUDENT

The instant you head off on a mission trip isn't the time for the key people in your life to yell, "Hasta la bye-bye!" and launch you into the world armed only with your Bible and a sleeping bag. Maybe you bought this book for yourself, but way more likely, someone put it in your hands to boost the quality of your mission trip experience.

So welcome to your trip—and to *Mission Trip Prep: A Student Journal for Capturing the Experience.* Wherever you're headed in your world, this book will help you get ready, to have a good trip close to God, and to help you come home. This book is your spot to start thinking about your experience, even if it's weeks or months into the future.

Jesus commanded us to go into all the world and make disciples (Matthew 28:18-20). You probably know that he predicted his people would go into the world filled with power (Acts 1:8). But there are still a couple questions: Why would he send you? And how can you make the most of your trip? This guide will help you grab Bible insights into why you're going, what you're doing, and how your project can be radically life-altering.

This book has three studies (1-3) to do at the start of your trip—better yet, before you go. There are six more (4-9) to do on your trip, and a final three (10-12) to do on your way home or after your trip. You can also flip to pages 74-75 to find Bible readings that fit your need and your mood.

The studies include questions meant to make you think. They also include simple questions to help you capture what you're thinking and feeling at the moment—both memories and Bible stuff—so that 10 years from now you have an accurate record of this pivotal event in your life. So put yourself into this book. Tuck it someplace safe when you get home. And for now, get ready for an adventure.

All God's Best,

Kevin Johnson

Kevin Johnson

GO.

CH.1

WHY GO?

WHY GO?

Unless you've been abducted by aliens—or bullied by a tambourine-wielding cult—you made a personal choice to be part of this mission trip. Rattling around in the back of your brain you have reasons for joining this fantastic adventure. Maybe you've thought a whole lot about what you expect of your trip. Or maybe not. Either way, pull up a mental picture of the best trip you could have. Then jot down some of what you're thinking about:

WHY AM I GOING?

HONESTLY, WHAT ARE THE TOP THREE REASONS YOU SIGNED UP FOR THIS TRIP?

_____

_____

_____

HOW DO YOU WANT TO CHANGE AND GROW THROUGH YOUR MISSION TRIP? IN OTHER WORDS, WHAT WOULD YOU LIKE GOD TO ACCOMPLISH IN YOU?

_____

_____

_____

HOW DO YOU WANT TO HELP OTHER PEOPLE—AND SHOW OFF GOD'S GREATNESS? WHAT DO YOU EXPECT GOD TO DO THROUGH YOU ON THIS TRIP?

_____

_____

_____

Being part of a mission project means having a huge wallop of fun. It also means getting swept up in something big beyond imagination. Look at what the Bible says:

> But you are a chosen people, a royal priesthood, a holy nation, a people belonging to God, that you may declare the praises of him who called you out of darkness into his wonderful light. Once you were not a people, but now you are the people of God; once you had not received mercy, but now you have received mercy.
>
> (1 Peter 2:9-10)

Chosen…royal…holy…belonging to God. Those words might sound huge—like they describe someone other than you. But they fit anyone who belongs to Jesus.

Being clear on those facts gives you huge reasons to go on your trip—and reasons to work hard at whatever you're planning to do. So ponder these:

How has God made you part of his people?

_____

_____

What does it mean that God has shown you mercy?

_____

_____

How has God called you out of darkness, busting you free from things you've done—or might have done without his presence in your life?

_____

_____

Roll all those thoughts together and answer this: What has God done in your life that's worth telling the world about through your words and actions?

_____

_____

God probably didn't rescue you from a life as an ax murderer or an acid-pushing drug dealer. But if God has been good to you—by bringing you into his family, yanking you from sin and selfishness—then you have something to share with the world. You have a reason to show the world who Jesus is.

WHAT AM I GETTING MYSELF INTO?

You have a picture in your mind of the place you'll be and the things you'll do on your trip. That picture, however, might have no resemblance to reality. There's no time like now to figure out what you're getting into. So jot your wonderings here—and remember to get the true scoop from your trip leaders!

What sounds great about your trip? (Do you think your expectations are realistic?)

_____

_____

_____

_____

_____

What sounds hard about the trip? What are you tense or fearful about?

_____

_____

_____

_____

_____

What questions do you want to ask your trip leaders about your trip?

_____

_____

_____

_____

_____

WRAP IT UP WITH PRAYER

God, thanks for giving me the chance to do this trip. Help me to get clear on why I'm going—both for the fun of hanging with my friends and for the big things you want to do in and through me.

DOING THE SE

RVANT THING

CH. 2

DOING THE SERVANT THING

You might have the idea that doing missions—this trip, for instance—guarantees your life will be jammed with wild joy. Well, sometimes. But serving isn't easy or automatic for any of us. So if you want to thrive on a mission project, the secret is knowing what the experience will cost—and being sure that whatever the price, doing the servant thing is worth it.

SO YOU WANT TO BE A SERVANT

You already know about servanthood—some good, some bad. Scribble what you know.

What's the biggest act of servanthood you've ever done? What did it accomplish?

_____

_____

_____

What small act of servanthood do you do on a regular basis? What good does it get done?

_____

_____

_____

When has giving of yourself—your time, energy, love, or money—brought you more hassles than happiness?

_____

_____

_____

One of the most astounding facts of the Bible is that the King of the Universe came to serve the human race. Jesus was totally God, yet he came to earth wrapped in human flesh. As you head out to serve your world, he's your one-of-a-kind example. Look at this:

> Your attitude should be the same that Christ Jesus had. Though he was God, he did not demand and cling to his rights as God. He made himself nothing; he took the humble position of a slave and appeared in human form. And in human form he obediently humbled himself even further by dying a criminal's death on a cross.
>
> (Philippians 2:5-8, NLT)

Get that picture? The status of Jesus was sky-high, yet he bowed to help our hurting world.

Jesus knew that service always carries a price. In fact, he said that whenever we follow him that we're wise to consider the cost (Luke 14:25-33). So don't duck out of thinking hard now about the price of servanthood.

How will your trip require you to be a servant? What will it cost you?

_____

_____

_____

_____

Need some help? Circle below anything that you think might personally challenge you about your trip. (Some might not fit your setting.) Then go back and add those to your list above.

✚ bunking in a tent, school, or church—with other people

✚ working hard and dripping sweat

✚ needing to follow cultural do's and don'ts

✚ doing jobs that don't seem fair or fun

✚ getting along with others

✚ lack of privacy

✚ heat or cold

✚ altitude

✚ working with teammates

✚ putting up with other people's attitudes

✚ having to share everything all the time

✚ strange, boring, or gross food

✚ racial and social prejudice

✚ grungy shared bathrooms

✚ lack of luxuries—deluxe cars, sound systems, computers, TVs, wardrobes

✚ pickpockets, theft, vandalism, violence

✚ lack of building materials or tools

+ lack of access to stores, groceries, and snacks-on-demand

+ seeing in-your-face evil

+ experiencing conflict with teammates and leaders

+ lack of dependable electricity, water, or communications

Know what? You're only happy paying the price of servanthood when you know that the price is worth paying. Look again at the example of Jesus. When he died on the cross for humankind's sins, he paid the ultimate price: his life. He didn't shrink from coughing up for that hefty bill because he had counted the cost and considered the effort worth it. Hebrews 12:2 tells us to get courage from that example of Jesus: "Let us fix our eyes on Jesus, the author and perfecter of our faith, who for the joy set before him endured the cross."

How can thinking about what Jesus did for you help you pay the price of serving others? What would your attitude be like if you imitated his way of looking at service?

_____

_____

_____

_____

_____

_____

_____

_____

THE PAYOFF OF BEING A SERVANT

Jesus looked past the pain of the cross and saw the swarms of people who would be saved by his actions. So what makes your trip worth the effort? What will your hard work accomplish for you, others, and God?

_____

_____

_____

_____

_____

_____

_____

_____

_____

If you have a hard time thinking of real benefits that will result from your hard work, chat with your team leaders. Get the inside story on the good that you're going to do.

WRAP IT UP WITH PRAYER

Jesus, when I get tired of the work we're doing on our trip, help me remember your example on the cross. And help me keep in the front of my brain the big goals we're working to accomplish.

CH. 3

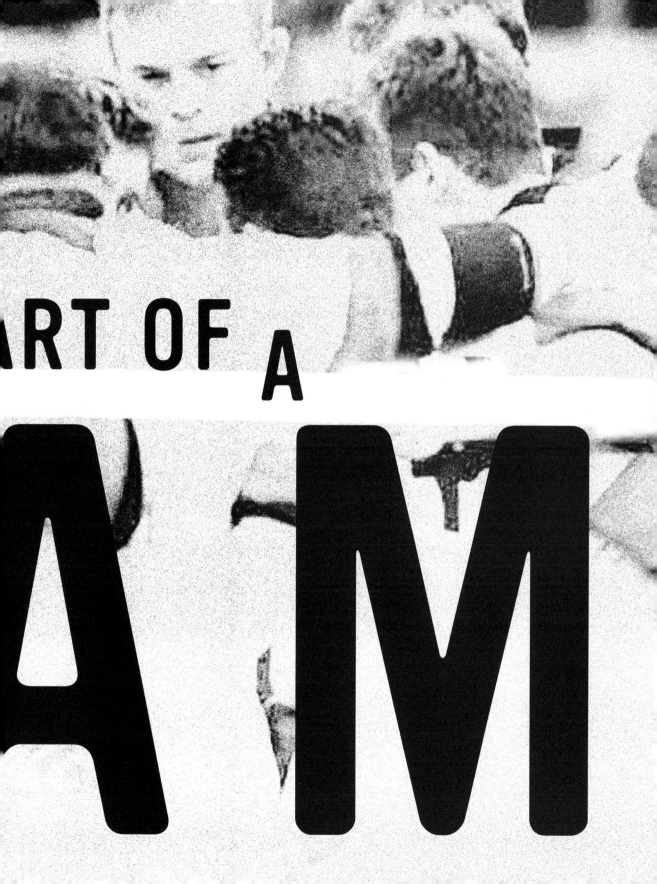

PART OF A TEAM

Not many generations ago, as missionaries prepared to sail for far-off lands, they packed their supplies in coffins. They knew that the only way they would ever get home was tucked inside those rough wooden boxes.

You won't face the same obstacles as missionaries who died of a ravaging jungle fever or wound up in cannibal soup. At the end of your trip you'll climb on a bus, on a plane, or into a minivan and be home in a blink. But you'll make sacrifices of your own—maybe sizable ones. And as you offer God your best, you'll be putting Romans 12:1 into action:

So brothers and sisters, since God has shown us great mercy, I beg you to offer your lives as a living sacrifice to him. Your offering must be only for God and pleasing to him, which is the spiritual way for you to worship (NCV).

Maybe you know that ultrafamous passage. But you might not have noticed that the next few verses make an unexpected twist. They inform you that whatever tough stuff you face as you worship God as a "living sacrifice," you get the help of your Christian sisters and brothers. Check this:

Just as our bodies have many parts and each part has a special function, so it is with Christ's body. We are all parts of his one body, and each of us has different work to do. And since we are all one body in Christ, we belong to each other, and each of us needs all the others.
(Romans 12:4-5, NLT)

Catch that reasoning? Right after Paul says that serving God means sacrifice, he reminds you that you get to serve him as part of a team. And here's the big point: He goes on to say that God has given Christians a mix of gifts that will make your team stronger—and make your service rock.

And that's huge. Whatever your gift is, God wants you to use it to the good of your team and your trip! So wrap your brain round this:

How scary would your project be if you all went without a team—if you all went solo?

_____

_____

_____

What can you accomplish together that you can't accomplish alone?

_____

_____

_____

YOUR GIFT TO YOUR TEAM

There's no doubt about it: You are an incredible gift to your team. Yet you might not believe that fact until you realize what you have to offer. So look through the list below and check the gifts you have to offer your team. Add others you think of.

(Some of these are what the Bible calls *spiritual gifts*. Others are qualities God wires into you at birth or builds into you through life experiences. All of them help your team function.)

- ☐ sense of humor
- ☐ enthusiasm
- ☐ determination
- ☐ understanding of God's goals
- ☐ music
- ☐ physical fitness and stamina
- ☐ art
- ☐ ability to work with kids

- ☐ construction skills
- ☐ evangelism
- ☐ steady emotions
- ☐ readiness to listen to others
- ☐ willingness to help in the background
- ☐ sports skills
- ☐ cooking
- ☐ teaching know-how
- ☐ cooperative attitude
- ☐ other _____
- ☐ other _____
- ☐ other _____
- ☐ other _____

How can you envision using your gifts to help your team accomplish its goals? Be specific!

_____

_____

_____

_____

_____

How can you show appreciation for the gifts others bring to your team?

_____

_____

_____

_____

_____

One more teammate thing: You might have signed up for a trip with a bunch of strangers. Or you might be going with people you, um, wish weren't going. You don't have to be a brain surgeon to realize that hostilities you bring to the trip can shred what your team is trying to accomplish. A couple questions:

What do you expect to be your biggest problem in getting along with your trip teammates?

_____

_____

_____

Is there anyone you need to get right with before the trip? How can you get your ugly issues solved now?

_____

_____

_____

If you need some short but smart guidance on how to work through problems with people, flip to **Relationship Solutions** on page 32.

WRAP IT UP WITH PRAYER

God, I need the other people my team. Without each other we won't accomplish everything you plan for us to do. Help me to use my unique gifts on the project and to encourage my teammates to use their gifts too.

MY TEAMMATES

Who is doing this trip with you? You might be going with a handful of people you know well—or a mob of strangers. As soon as you know who your teammates are, jot down their names here.

_____

_____

_____

_____

_____

_____

Find out how you can pray for them and scribble those needs down as well.

_____

_____

_____

_____

_____

_____

_____

Ask them about their favorite junk food so you can pack loads for the trip.

_____

_____

_____

Tape a team picture here if you've got one, so you can learn names before you leave. If you already know everyone's name, then challenge yourself to talk to each person before the trip by finding out and recording one miscellaneous factoid about each person.

_____

_____

_____

_____

_____

RELATIONSHIP SOLUTIONS

A huge part of your trip—whether your project is bad or a blast—has to do with people. if you have problems getting along with any of your teammates, you owe it to yourself and your team to work out your difficulties as quickly as you can.

Even when teammates are grotesquely annoying, lots of times they're doing something different, not wrong. When you stew about your relationship problems, think about these three bits of wisdom from the Bible:

✚ **YOU MIGHT HAVE A PROBLEM OF YOUR OWN TO DEAL WITH.** Jesus pointed out that it's easy to miss our own huge faults while we hunt down the small faults of others. Listen up: "Why do you notice the little piece of dust in your friend's eye, but you don't notice the big piece of wood in your own eye? How can you say to your friend, 'Let me take that little piece of dust out of your eye'? Look at yourself! You still have that big piece of wood in your own eye. You hypocrite!"

Jesus finishes with some pointed advice: "First, take the wood out of your own eye. Then you will see clearly to take the dust out of your friend's eye" (Matthew 7:3-5, NCV).

Don't miss the message: Fess up to your part of a problem before you make a fuss.

✚ **FORGETTING A SMALL OFFENSE CAN BE AN OKAY THING TO DO.** "Love covers over a multitude of sins," Peter wrote (1 Peter 4:8). You don't have to fake that a hurt didn't happen, but aim to cut others the same slack you want them to cut you. Jesus said people will judge you with the same amount of ugliness you dish out at them (Matthew 7:2).

✚ If you still have a problem to solve, aim to work it out in love. In Matthew 18:15-17 Jesus lays out three smart steps for solving issues with people who have wronged you—steps you might find handy now or on the trip:

1. Talk directly with the person about what he or she did wrong.
2. If that doesn't work, bring along someone trustworthy to help you reason with your teammate.
3. If that still doesn't solve your difficulty, your next step is to "tell it to the church." That doesn't mean resorting to wicked gossip but to getting help from your team leaders or other mature Christians leaders in your life.

Paul adds another smart point: Whenever you need to say tough things to others, put love at the core of your conversation (Ephesians 4:15). Your goal isn't to destroy an enemy but to win back a friend (Matthew 18:15).

As you contemplate the right way to get along as a group, look first to the Bible for direction. Check out **Unfuzzy Love** (page 64) for all sorts of Bible commands for working as a team.

GOD'S MASTER PIECE

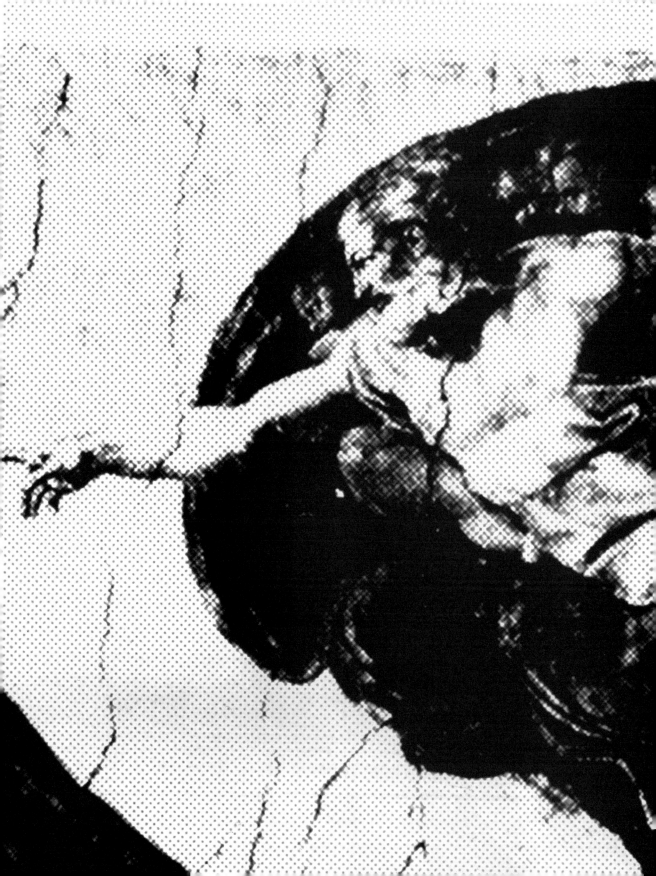

CH. **4**

GOD'S MASTERPIECE

Launching into a mission trip is like pausing at the bottom of a mountain you'd like to climb. Looks fun. But you aren't sure you can wheeze your way all the way to the top. Sure, you finger-painted in kindergarten—but you've never prepped and painted a house. Or you've studied the Bible at church—but you've never shared your faith with a stranger. Can you really pull off what you came to do?

How are you feeling about starting? Scribble down three things you think or feel about this trip right now.

_____

_____

_____

Your first day might be exciting—or excruciating. Whatever you're feeling—confident, scared, stumped—here's the truth: God designed you for the job you have to do. Check this Bible passage:

God saved you by his special favor when you believed. And you can't take credit for this; it is a gift from God. Salvation is not a reward for the good things we have done, so none of us can boast about it. For we are God's masterpiece. He has created us anew in Christ Jesus, so that we can do the good things he planned for us long ago.

(Ephesians 2:8-10 NLT)

DATE:_____ **SOMETHING I DID TODAY:**_____

God loves you extravagantly. And he will equip you totally for whatever comes your way on your trip. That passage says that you don't score points with God because you serve him through missions. God has already saved you, accepting you totally and giving you a relationship with him that starts now and lasts forever. But it also says he has a plan for you:

THE TRUTH ABOUT YOU

Fill in the blanks from verse 10 of that passage:

I am God's _____. He created me _____ in Christ so I

can do_____that he planned for me _____.

Your Bible version might say that you are God's workmanship, and that's true. But the word literally means poem or work of art or, better yet, masterpiece.

God says you are his masterpiece. What do you think of that fact?

_____

_____

_____

_____

_____

_____

SOMETHING I SAW TODAY:_____

Even though you're God's masterpiece, you're not going on your trip to hang on a wall. Let's get practical. Figure out these true-false statements:

The fact that God handcrafted me guarantees that this trip will be…

T F The easiest thing I've ever done.
T F The most fascinating work of my life.
T F The most fun I'll ever have until the day I die.

Bonehead! If you marked any of those true, kick those thoughts out of your head right now. Being God's masterpiece doesn't mean you won't struggle, get bored, or need to learn new skills. But God has had good jobs planned for you from "long ago." And this project is part of his plan.

Easy question: Now that you're settling in, what exactly did you come here to do?

_____

_____

_____

Tougher question: What are your concrete goals for what you want to do during your trip? Think ahead to the day you go home. How will you know you've done your job well? If you can, set three specific goals you want to accomplish by the time you leave.

_____

_____

_____

_____

SOMETHING I LAUGHED AT TODAY:_____

God thinks you're capable of doing this trip well, or he wouldn't have called you to this task. But when you feel queasy or uneasy, tell God. Ask him to work through you. And talk to your trip leaders about your uncertainties.

WEIRD STUFF I DID ON THIS TRIP

Your trip leaders probably laid out a pretty brochure that told you all the things you would do on your trip. But they didn't tell you that you might wipe a kid's snotty nose with your bare hands…demolish a wall with a sledgehammer…share your faith with a blind guy…haul your own water to force a toilet to flush.

You don't want to forget those once-in-a-lifetime moments. So every time you get to do something strange—big or small—come back here and write it down.

_____

_____

_____

_____

_____

WRAP IT UP WITH PRAYER

God, thanks for making me your masterpiece and trusting me to serve you. Help me to carry out everything you have planned for me to do.

SOMETHING I LEARNED TODAY:_____

GRAT
UDE

TUDE

ATTI

CH. 5

GRATITUDE ATTITUDE

Face it. If your project was purely about having fun, everyone in your hometown would have signed up, and you'd have a bazillion people on your trip. But most mission trips stretch you to do new things. Hard things. Things you never saw coming. Are you ready for anything?

THINK BACK

What did you have to do yesterday that you really didn't feel like doing?

_____

_____

How did you react to the request—or order—to do that?

_____

_____

_____

DATE: _____ **SOMETHING I DID TODAY:**_____

Maybe you were a total saint and did everything asked of you. Then answer this: Did you witness anyone else displaying a less-than-marvelous attitude toward their tasks? What did you see?

_____

_____

_____

Suppose your mission trip leaders want you to do something. How would you prefer that they motivate you?

    a. Threaten to break my thumbs if I don't do it.
    b. Call my parents so they can help my leaders turn up the heat.
    c. Make me whimper about all the people in the world who have less than I do.
    d. Persuade me of the right thing to do and give me the power to do it.

There's no better way than the last choice, and God knows it. When he wants you to do something, he doesn't send out an angel to threaten to bust a body part. He looks for willing hearts. And God empowers you to reach the greatest goal imaginable: introducing people to Jesus Christ.

Whatever it is you're doing on your trip—construction, street evangelism, social action—you have the ultimate goal of helping people recognize Jesus as their Messiah and Master. Look at how the apostle Paul describes your purpose:

> Through Christ, God made peace between us and himself, and God gave us the work of telling everyone about the peace we can have with him. God was in Christ, making peace between the world and himself. In Christ, God did not hold the world guilty of its sins. And he gave us this message of peace. So we have been sent to speak for Christ. It is as if God is calling to you through us. We speak for Christ when we beg you to be at peace with God (2 Corinthians 5:18-20, NCV).

SOMETHING I SAW TODAY:_____

You're not just God's masterpiece. You're also his ambassador. By every good word you utter and every good action you do, you communicate his message of peace through Christ's death on the cross. That's your big purpose. But God doesn't just hand you a job. He gives you power from the inside to do it—and maybe in a way you don't expect.

WHY DO *THAT?*

Sooner or later someone will want you to explain your project—not just what you're doing but *why.* So answer: *Why* are you on this trip?

_____

_____

Here's a related question: Why makes this project something you want to do instead of something you have to do? What makes this trip cool for you?

_____

_____

_____

Right before the Bible passage you just read, Paul points out why you work for God. Read on:

Whatever we do, it is because Christ's love controls us. Since we believe that Christ died for everyone, we also believe that we have all died to the old life we used to live. He died for everyone so that those who receive his new life will no longer live to please themselves. Instead, they will live to please Christ, who died and was raised for them.

(2 Corinthians 5:14-15, NLT)

SOMETHING I LAUGHED AT TODAY:_____

Say it in your own words: What would make you want to serve God gladly?

_____

_____

Ponder this: No one can rise to the challenges of your trip for you. Serving God with all your heart is totally your choice. And enthusiastic service only happens when you grasp the greatness of God's love for you—especially the love Christ showed on the cross. Love is what powers you up to please Christ.

GETTING MY HEART ON TRACK

God wants you jazzed about your job—whatever it is. How that happens isn't a mystery. It often starts by talking to God and telling him two things:

1. I'M GRATEFUL, GOD, FOR YOUR LOVE—FOR EVERYTHING YOU'VE DONE FOR ME.

2. I'M GRATEFUL, GOD, FOR THIS OPPORTUNITY TO LOVE YOU BACK AND TO DEMONSTRATE YOUR LOVE TO OTHERS.

Take some time to tell God those things right now. And whenever you ask him to help you serve him gladly—because you want to, not because you have to—be sure that's a request he's overjoyed to answer.

WRAP IT UP WITH PRAYER

Jesus, I want to serve you with every bit of my heart. Fill me with gratitude to you. I'm serving you today because I want to.

SOMETHING I LEARNED TODAY: _____

CH. **6**

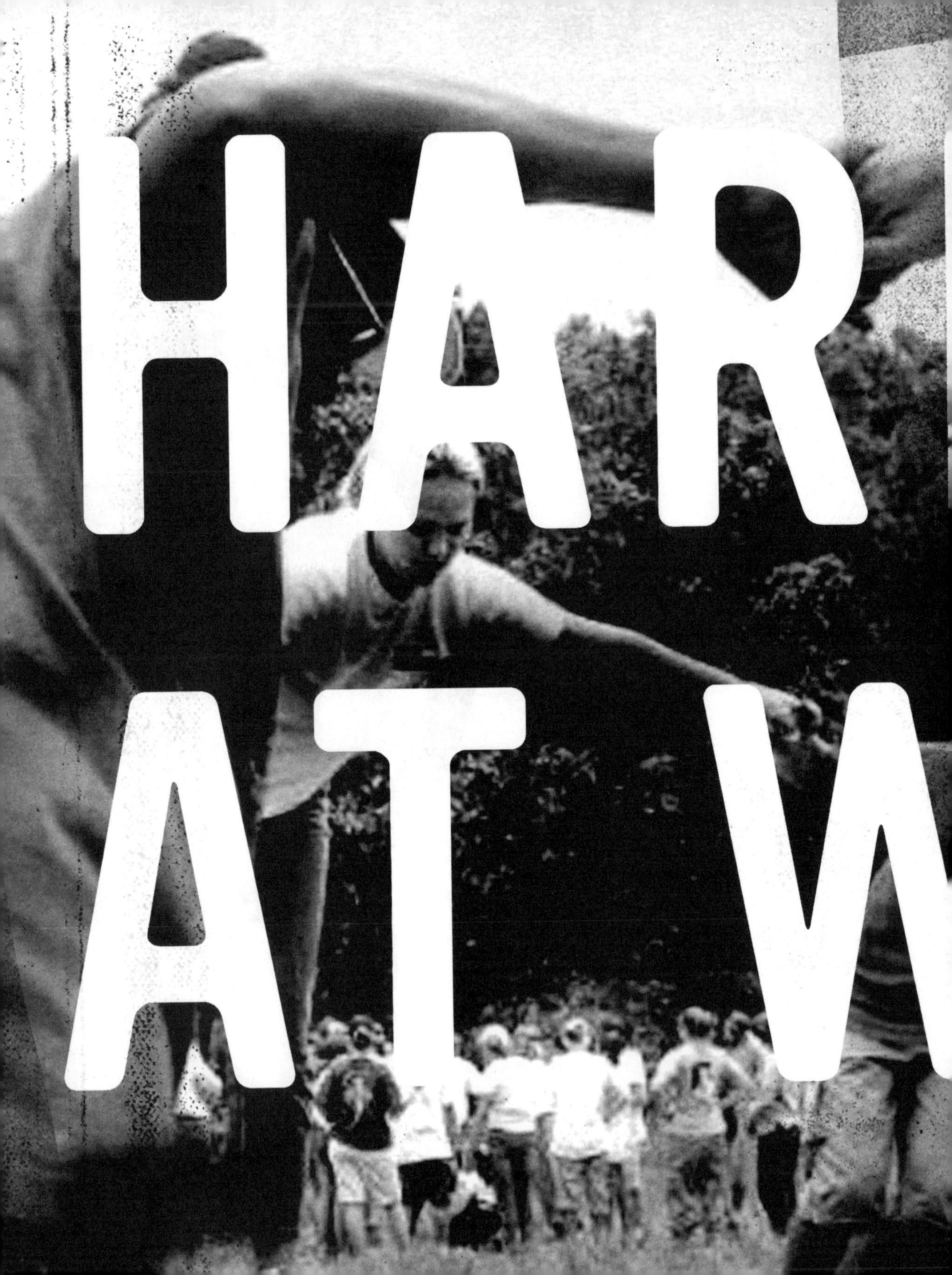
HAR
ATW

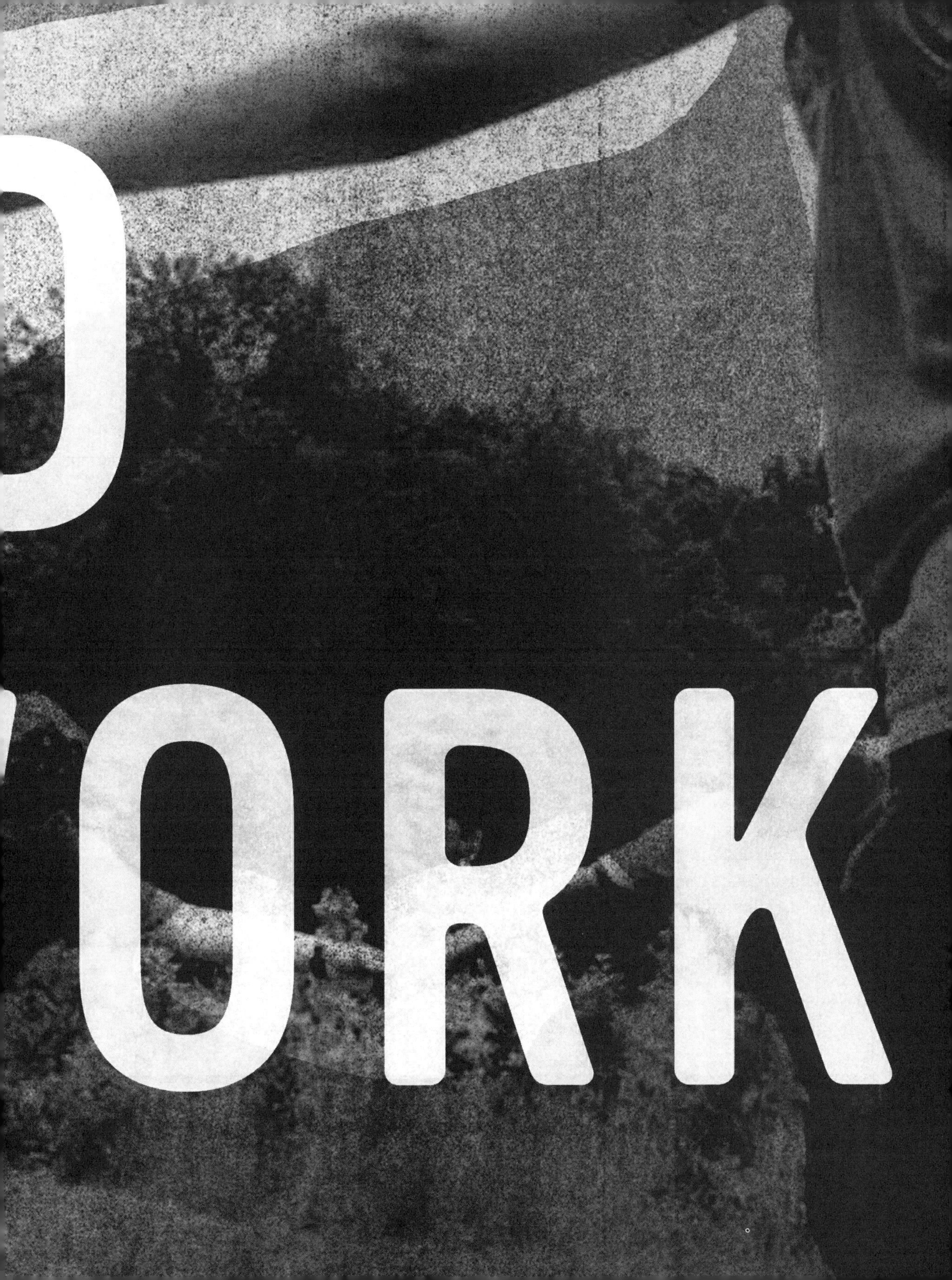
ORK

HARD AT WORK

God made you his masterpiece. He injects love into your heart to motivate you. So what happens if that massively motivated giftedness stays jammed up inside you? It melts into a warm-fuzzy, group-hug mush. It rots into a wish that the world would be a kinder, nicer place. But God aims to give your giftedness an outlet. He called you to your trip to get things done. So what does love look like when it gets into gear?

SLACK-O-METER

Ponder that question while you take this quiz. You're a ways into your project. Be brutally honest about yourself as you score yourself from 1 to 10 on each of these statements. How hard have you been working?

a. I could be a cover model for *Slacker* magazine. ____
b. I whine. A lot. ____
c. I work so slowly that once or twice an hour I fall over and quit working altogether. ____
d. I make busywork look important. ____
e. I watch like a hawk to make sure I don't exert myself any more or less than anyone else. ____
f. I put my nose to the grindstone but I don't have any fun. ____
g. I stay focused and on-task most of the time. ____
h. I worry that other people think I'm trying to make them look bad. ____
i. I work as hard as I know how. ____
j. I push myself beyond what I think I'm capable of. And I'm loving it. ____

My score (total of all your ratings) ____.

DATE: _____ **SOMETHING I DID TODAY:** _____

One big question: Are you happy with your score? Why or why not?

_____

_____

You might not feel like giving your all to the tasks at hand when your job is to do stuff you don't feel like doing… or no one else seems to be working… or your leaders are being bozos… or the people you serve don't seem grateful. But wholehearted work doesn't pick and choose when to do its best—or not.

MORE SLACKER QUESTIONS

You're already working harder than anyone else—and then your team leader dives in with another assignment for you. How do you react?

_____

_____

You want to quit doing whatever it is you're supposed to be doing—and there's not a leader in sight. What do you do?

_____

_____

If you're ever swallowed up by a bad attitude about working hard, how could it help recharge you to remember why you're here?

_____

_____

SOMETHING I SAW TODAY:_____

When you're tempted to give your project your less-than-best, how could you remind yourself why your efforts matter?

_____

_____

Remember? Being convinced that your project has real-life impact is a big part of keeping going when the going gets nasty. But there's another piece to getting love into gear. Even when you know your project is important, you still need a way to measure if you're pouring on your best.

Lots of people don't know what hard work looks like—or feels like. But Colossians 3:22-24 paints a vivid picture. Check this:

> Do not obey just when they are watching you, to gain their favor, but serve them honestly, because you respect the Lord. In all the work you are doing, work the best you can. Work as if you were doing it for the Lord, not for people. Remember that you will receive your reward from the Lord, which he promised to his people. You are serving the Lord Christ. (NCV)

Paul wrote those verses to slaves, but get a couple things clear: First, taking part in a mission trip doesn't make you a slave. Second, if you're curious, Paul wasn't defending slavery. The slavery of his times was more like indentured servitude in the modern world. But his words still pry open our eyes to how we can give our best to God.

What does that passage say real work looks like? List at least four traits:

1. _____

2. _____

3. _____

4. _____

SOMETHING I LAUGHED AT TODAY:_____

AM I WORKING HARD OR HARDLY WORKING?

You can make Colossians 3:22-24 totally practical by using it as a guide to come up with your own concrete tests that you can use today to tell whether you're working your hardest. Make each of them start with "I will...." The first one is done to give you an example.

TEST 1   I will work hard whether or not other people are watching.

TEST 2   I will...

_____

_____

_____

TEST 3   I will...

_____

_____

_____

WRAP IT UP WITH PRAYER

God, open my eyes so I can tell if I'm working hard or hardly working. I want to apply myself to giving my best to you in whatever I do.

SOMETHING I LEARNED TODAY:_____

CH.7

SHOULDER

SHOULDER

CH. 7

SHOULDER-TO-SHOULDER

When you head home, your mission trip team might leave behind a beautifully rehabbed house. Or you might have pulled-off a jaw-dropping evangelistic outreach. Yet the Bible boldly says that what you leave behind might actually be a pile of trash. No matter how great your accomplishments look, the lack of one indispensable thing can make your whole trip stink.

Just like the Bible gives you a test of what real work looks like, it also gives you a test of whether work is really as good as it looks. Try this:

> If I speak in the tongues of men and of angels, but have not love, I am only a resounding gong or a clanging cymbal. If I have the gift of prophecy and can fathom all mysteries and all knowledge, and if I have a faith that can move mountains, but have not love, I am nothing. If I give all I possess to the poor and surrender my body to the flames, but have not love, I gain nothing.
>
> (1 Corinthians 13:1-3)

According to that passage, what makes your trip truly great?_____

_____

Why would losing sight of that one thing do such damage to your project?

_____

_____

DATE: _____ **SOMETHING I DID TODAY:**_____

Just to be clear, who all do you get to show that one thing to on your trip?

_____

_____

_____

Hmmm…if that one thing is key to the success of your service to God, how do you define love?

_____

_____

_____

That's a huge question, and you could argue that it takes the whole Bible to answer. But you get a start in the verses that fall right after the passage you just read. These words from the Bible's "love chapter" define love like this:

> Love is patient, love is kind. It does not envy, it does not boast, it is not proud. It is not rude, it is not self-seeking, it is not easily angered, it keeps no record of wrongs. Love does not delight in evil but rejoices with the truth. It always protects, always trusts, always hopes, always perseveres.
>
> (1 Corinthians 13:4-7)

If love is so utterly important to your trip, do you have any concrete ideas of how you can show love today? Think of at least three actions you can do and jot them here. Attach a name or names to the Christlike thing you aim to do.

_____

_____

SOMETHING I SAW TODAY:_____

UNFUZZY LOVE

Still feel fuzzy on what love can look like? Look at this list fished from Ephesians, chapters 4-5. You can use it as a checklist for getting along—and to add ideas to your list above.

+ Be humble and gentle (4:2)

+ Make room for each other's faults (4:2)

+ Stay unified (4:3)

+ Rid yourself of bad habits of body and mind (4:22-23)

+ Let the new you being remade by God shine through (4:24)

+ Speak truthfully to your teammates (4:25)

+ Don't let the sun set while you are still angry (4:26)

+ Don't swipe what isn't yours (4:28)

+ Share with the needy (4:28)

+ Pick words that encourage others (4:29)

+ Ditch bitterness, rage, and anger (4:31)

+ Stop wishing the worst for people (4:31)

+ Be kind and compassionate to one another (4:32)

SOMETHING I LAUGHED AT TODAY:_____

✝ Forgive others like God forgives you (4:32).

✝ Flee sexual sins—along with obscenity or crude jokes (5:3-4)

The end of that passage sums it up what love looks like—and how you can love because God has loved you:

Be imitators of God, therefore, as dearly loved children and live a life of love, just as Christ loved us and gave himself up for us as a fragrant offering and sacrifice to God.
(Ephesians 5:1-2)

Don't look at that list as a reason to shred yourself. But in that list you probably see a specific way you can work on getting along with your teammates, trip leaders, and the people you serve.

So think hard: What's your biggest struggle to get along with people on the trip so far?

_____

_____

What can you do today to work on that one area—to solve it in a way that pleases God?

_____

_____

WRAP IT UP WITH PRAYER

God, I know that the things I do on this trip are important. But I know that how I do them matters even more. Help me to love everyone I meet today—my teammates, my leaders, the people we serve.

SOMETHING I LEARNED TODAY:_____

CH.**8**

FINISHING

STRONG

CH.**8**

FINISHING STRONG

Every mission trip is a race. You might be in a sprint—where you pour everything you've got into, say, a three-day outreach. Or you could be in a month-long marathon—where you need to pace yourself lest you become a wasted ball of quivering flesh stranded on the roadside. If you're on week-long trip, you're hoofing it toward the end of your project.

    Wherever you're at, you might feel like you've picked a good pace toward the finish. But if ever the sun gets hot, your teammates crabby, or the work unbearable, you might be wondering how you can run strong to the end. The great news is this: God never leaves you to run your race alone.

What kind of strength do you think you need to get through today—and to thrive through the rest of your trip?

_____

_____

_____

Where can you get that kind of help?_____

_____

_____

DATE: _____ **SOMETHING I DID TODAY:**_____

There are a million ways you can recharge. But get this: Ultimately there is only one source of your strength. Check this promise from Isaiah 40:31:

> But those who hope in the Lord will renew their strength. They will soar on wings like eagles; they will run and not grow weary, they will walk and not be faint.

Exactly who gets to wing like an eagle, trot and not drop, walk and not fall over?

_____

_____

_____

That's the promise of God to anyone who relies on him. But God makes an even more specific promise to you as you carry his message to the world. Grab a look at Acts 1:8. That's where Jesus told his disciples,

> You will receive power when the Holy Spirit comes on you; and you will be my witnesses in Jerusalem, and in all Judea and Samaria, and to the ends of the earth.

So what does Acts 1:8 promise you? How do you get that? _____

_____

_____

What does God count on you doing with what he gives you?

_____

_____

_____

SOMETHING I SAW TODAY:_____

God will always give you what you need to do the tasks on your trip. Hudson Taylor, a great missionary to China, once said, "God's work done in God's way will never lack God's supply."

TAPPING GOD'S POWER

You'd probably like a gob of power from God—an infusion of strength that fires up your attitudes, sharpens your actions, and makes you stronger than you ever thought possible. Yet you might think that getting hold of God's strength is only for great believers of the Bible or for gutsy missionaries in the old days.

The two verses you just read prove that God has power available to you right now. You might expect his power to arrive in a mysterious zap that makes you a better Christian or a radically gung-ho team member. But God usually recharges us in down-to-earth ways, giving us more of his Spirit as we get close to him. There are simple things God makes available to you that will give you the boost you need to keep serving him enthusiastically.

How could you make the most of each of these God-given rechargers to get strength today? Try to jot an idea for each:

teammates _____

leaders _____

my Bible _____

prayer _____

exercise _____

time by myself _____

worship _____

free time _____

SOMETHING I LAUGHED AT TODAY:_____

Which of those things sound like just what you need? Which one do you need most? And what's your plan to make use of that recharger today?

_____

_____

_____

_____

Keep in mind that grabbing hold of God's strength doesn't mean all your problems on a trip—or in life—will go away. Even the strongest of God's servants get tired. Paul described it like this:

> But we have this treasure in jars of clay to show that this all-surpassing power is from God and not from us. We are hard pressed on every side, but not crushed; perplexed, but not in despair; persecuted, but not abandoned; struck down, but not destroyed.
>
> (2 Corinthians 4:7-9)

Paul faced unending troubles as he sought to spread the Good News of Christ. But because he got strength from God, he was the guy who could always press on. He could say,

> I can do everything through him who gives me strength. (Philippians 4:13)

If you're looking for strength from the Bible but don't know where to start, flip a page and check out "Need More to Read?"

WRAP IT UP WITH PRAYER

God, I need your power to get me through today. I can't do all the tasks on this trip in my own strength. Show me how to rely on you in every moment of my day.

SOMETHING I LEARNED TODAY:_____

NEED MORE TO READ?

Maybe you're on a long trip. Or your team has been marooned on a desert island, and you've run out of things to read in your Bible. Or maybe you've got an itch the studies in this book just aren't scratching. Here's a stack of top places in the Bible to start reading. So pick a topic and dig in.

LOVE 1 John 4:7-21, Galatians 5:13-15, 1 Corinthians 13

YOUR MOUTH James 3:1-12, Ephesians 4:29-32, Ephesians 5:4-5

ANGER Ephesians 4:26-27

MAKING CHOICES Proverbs 3:5-8, James 4:13-17

BEING SURE YOU'RE A CHRISTIAN John 3:1-21, Romans 10:9-10, John 5:24

HOW GOD STICKS CLOSE TO YOU Romans 8:31-39, Hebrews 13:5-6, Joshua 1:9, Psalm 23

HANGING CLOSE TO GOD James 4:7, Hebrews 4:14-16, Philippians 3:7-14

TOUGH TIMES James 1:6-7, Romans 8:18, 1 Peter 1:3-9, Lamentations 3:19-25

FRIENDS 1 John 4:7-8, Ephesians 5:15-21, Hebrews 10:23-25, Hebrews 3:12-13

GUY-GIRL RELATIONSHIPS Proverbs 30:18-19, Job 31:1-4, Hebrews 13:4, 1 Thessalonians 4:3-8

TIREDNESS AND STRESS Isaiah 40:30-31, Philippians 4:6-8

DOING WRONG Romans 3:23, Romans 6:23

THE HOLY SPIRIT Galatians 5:16-25, Romans 8:1-17

PARENTS Ephesians 6:1-4

SCHOOL Ephesians 6:5-9, Ecclesiastes 12:11-13

STUFF Philippians 4:19, Matthew 6:19-34

FAMILY TROUBLES BACK HOME Psalm 27:10, Psalm 62:1-2

OBEDIENCE 1 John 2:1-6, James 4:7, Hebrews 3:6-19, 1 Peter 1:13-16

WHY BOTHER READING THE BIBLE Romans 15:4, 2 Timothy 3:16-17, Psalm 119:105

REJECTION Psalm 138:6-7, Matthew 5:11-12, Hebrews 13:6

DATING 2 Corinthians 6:14-18, 1 Corinthians 13:4-8, 1 Thessalonians 4:3-8

PRIDE James 3:13-18, Galatians 5:26

MAKING GOD HAPPY Deuteronomy 10:12-13, Micah 6:8

SHARING YOUR FAITH Acts 1:8, Matthew 28:18-20

FEELING INFERIOR Isaiah 62:3-4, Isaiah 43:4, Hebrews 2:6-7

BIG SHOTS Romans 13:1-7

DEPRESSION Psalm 42, 2 Corinthians 1:3-11

KNOWING GOD IS REAL John 7:16-17, 1 Corinthians 15:1-19

CELEBRATING THAT YOU FEEL GOOD Philippians 4:4, Psalm 100, Psalm 150

CH. 9

REASON TO

PAI

CH. 9

REASON TO PARTY

It's an astonishing truth: Because Christ died for you and rose, God's acceptance of you is so total that there's nothing you can do to earn his love or wow him—even going on a mission trip. But that doesn't mean you haven't accomplished some intensely incredible things. Because God has been at work through you, you've carried out God's plans. You've seen God act in ways David summed up in Psalm 40:5:

> Lord my God, you have done many miracles.
> Your plans for us are many.
> If I tried to tell them all,
> there would be too many to count. (NCV)

You might have a dark side of your brain telling you that whatever you did, it wasn't good enough—that you didn't help enough people, pound enough nails, or pass out enough evangelistic tracts. But if you've served with all your heart, God says, "Excellent! You are a good servant" (Matthew 25:23).

STUFF WORTH CELEBRATING

What you and your friends have accomplished is worth multiple high-fives and back slaps. Take a bit of time to remember and record some of the great stuff God did on your project.

DATE:_____ **SOMETHING I DID TODAY:**_____

My favorite memories about this trip

_____

_____

_____

_____

The things about this trip I wish would never end

_____

_____

_____

_____

Think hard for this one: Five things I'm proud we accomplished

_____

_____

_____

_____

_____

SOMETHING I SAW TODAY:_____

You accomplished concrete, visible things. But you can't see some of your biggest feats—like the good growth that happened inside you as you followed God's long-ago plans. That inside job is exactly what Psalm 40 talks about next:

> You [God] do not want sacrifices and offerings. But you have made a hole in my ear to show that my body and life are yours…My God, I want to do what you want. Your teachings are in my heart.
>
> (Psalm 40:6-8, NCV)

God designed you to be a living sacrifice, not to toast animals as an offering for sin. He wants you to want what he wants. But what's up with jabbing a hole in your ear?

Back in the Old Testament, a servant who loved his master and volunteered to be permanently bound to him got his ear pierced—with an awl (Exodus 21:5-6). It was a sign that his whole life belonged to his master. That's what Paul meant when he called himself—and others—a *bondslave*, being God's totally available servant.

What have you learned about being a willing servant on your project?

_____

_____

_____

What have you seen God do in you? How have you changed?

_____

_____

_____

SOMETHING I LAUGHED AT TODAY:_____

What has God done through you as you served?

_____

_____

_____

Your hard work on your project gives you tons to celebrate. And if your trip inched you closer to serving God like a bondservant—with your whole heart for your whole life—that should rocket to the top of your reasons to party!

NOTES TO SELF

Two months or 10 years from now you could be left with fuzzy memories of your project—unless you jot some notes to remind you what you're thinking right now. You can use the space at the back of this book to journal wads more, but fill out your thoughts right now for starters.

A big experience, feeling, or new thought I never want to forget

_____

_____

_____

_____

_____

_____

SOMETHING I LEARNED TODAY:_____

Something I want to say to my parents when I get home

_____

_____

_____

What I learned about why I need other Christians

_____

_____

_____

What it means to me to continue serving God with every bit of my heart

_____

_____

_____

WRAP IT UP WITH PRAYER

God, I'm glad for the things we accomplished on this project as we worked hard together. I'm really thankful for the growth you've caused in me and for bringing me closer to you.

STICKING TIGH

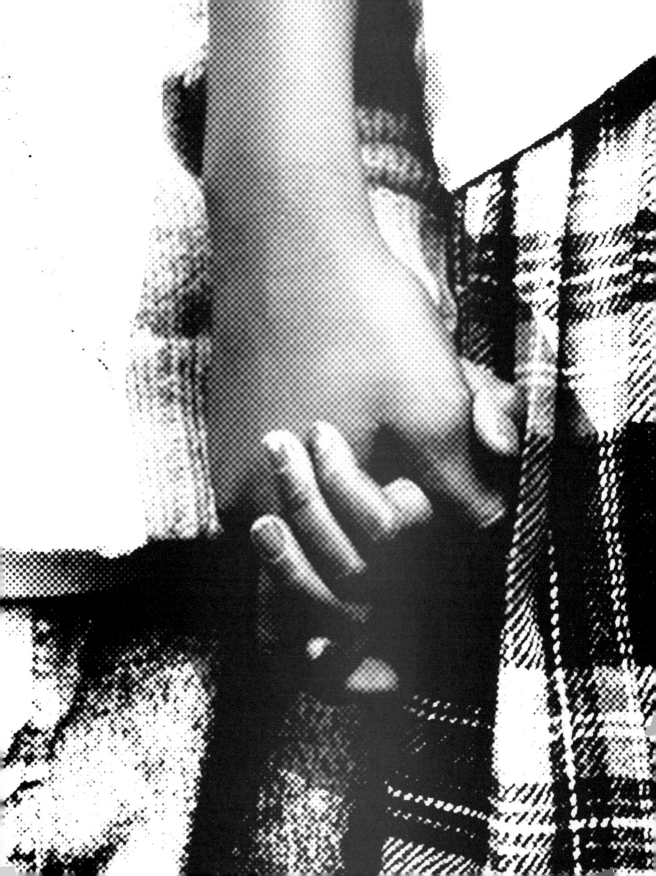

CH. 10

STICKING TIGHT

It's a slam-dunk sure thing that at your high school graduation one of the speakers will waddle up to the microphone and say "This is the last time we'll all be together!" And unless you graduate with less than a dozen people—a dozen people who really like each other enough to stay in touch—they'll be absolutely right.

You can count on this truth: Once you go home, your group won't ever be the same. You've had—hopefully—a mind-blowing experience together. But you're going back to everyday life. Some of your teammates are likely heading into unhappy family situations and unhealthy peer influences. Maybe you are.

You might feel right now like you could never forget your trip. But the feelings you kindle on a trip blow out as easily a match in stiff wind. The real job of your trip is just beginning. Your task is to keep the experience of your trip alive—and to fan the flame of everything you learned.

Wonder how? Hebrews 10:24-25 hands you a huge hint. Right after it informs you that you have the right as a Christian to run boldly into God's presence—one of the coolest promises in the entire Bible—it tells you that your priority is to keep your Christian friendships tight:

Think of ways to encourage one another to outbursts of love and good deeds. And let us not neglect our meeting together, as some people do, but encourage and warn each other. (NLT)

Which of those instructions sound fun—and easy?

_____

_____

_____

Do any of those commands sound hard—or even harsh? Which ones?

_____

_____

_____

_____

_____

_____

Supporting each other…encouraging each other to outbursts of good deeds…those are reasonably easy if you make the effort. That warning thing sounds tough. Think about how those things can happen.

What are three ways you can keep on boosting your teammates—and get powered up yourself—once you're home?

1. _____

2. _____

3. _____

Name two places and times each week you will commit to keep meeting together. Your meetings don't have to be at church, though that's a basic place to start. You can do lunch at school, pray over breakfast, get deep over late-night pizza run. But your goal isn't simply hanging out—it's staying spiritually ablaze.

1. _____

2. _____

Warning—and being warned—is one of the hardest things you'll do in your Christian life. But it's how you keep your spiritually life from getting snuffed. So who is one person you'll continue to let into your life in a deep way—by letting them warn you if you're wandering away from Jesus? How will that accountability happen?

_____

_____

_____

If you want to keep a fire burning, you keep the coals close to each other. It's simple: If you spread out, your flame burns out.

WRAP IT UP WITH PRAYER

God, thanks for giving us a great trip. Help my teammates and me stick tight to each other and hang on to everything we've learned.

MY BIGGEST, BEST, AND BADDEST

My funniest moment

_____

_____

_____

My team leader's weirdest moment

_____

_____

My toughest moment

_____

_____

_____

The most disturbing thing I saw (maybe poverty, violence, racism)

_____

_____

_____

A team member's most annoying habit

_____

_____

My teammate most likely to become a life-long missionary

_____

My most significant moment—the one that puts the whole trip in a nutshell

_____

_____

_____

SPOTTING
YOUR M

ISSION

SPOTTING YOUR MISSION

God didn't design you to go backward in life:

...to walk, then go back to crawling.
...to get over an illness, then get knocked flat again.
...to get teeth straightened, then watch them *fuh-whang* back.

The saddest situations in life feel like you've climbed out of a hole, then slid back to where you started.

The ghastliest thing that can happen after any project is to go back to life as usual. If that's not what you want, then you need to figure why your trip did you good—and how to bring your experience home.

So what about your trip helped you grow spiritually?

_____

_____

_____

That's not tough to answer. You grow when you're with Christian friends. You grow when you see your world and the Bible in freshly eye-popping ways. What makes a mission project a one-of-kind shot at growth, however, is that you serve big-time—hour after hour, day after day.

Service is indispensable to your Christian life. It's not something you do on your trip, then fling aside like a used-up bottle of sunscreen. If you want to keep growing, service has to become part of your everyday routine.

That's what the apostle Paul discovered when he met Jesus in a high-voltage spiritual experience:
As he neared Damascus on his journey, suddenly a light from heaven flashed around him.

He fell to the ground and heard a voice say to him, "Saul, Saul, why do you persecute me?"

"Who are you, Lord?" Saul asked.

"I am Jesus, whom you are persecuting," he replied. "Now get up and go into the city, and you will be told what you must do." (Acts 9:3-6)

Interesting fact: After that spiritual jolt, God didn't send Paul out to preach to the crowds of the Roman Empire. He sent him off to practice in an out-of-the-way place (Galatians 1:11-23).

You might dream you could go back to the electrifying experience you had on your trip. But unless your parents spring you from school and ship you back to your project, God has a different plan in store. He aims for you to practice ministering to others right where you're at.

Why? Because serving God is like any other skill. It takes practice. That practice happens not just on once-a-year mission trips but at home. Home is the only setting in the world where you can make service part of everyday life. It's time to think hard about how you can serve right here, right now.

So think back to your trip. What tasks were actually fun—and you'd like to do more?

_____

_____

_____

Which jobs were the hardest—and you wouldn't mind avoiding?

_____

_____

_____

How can you do that same kind of work at home—right here, right now?

_____

_____

_____

PREFERENCES AND POSSIBILITIES

Even if you loved what you did on your project, you might be ready for something new. And your setting might provide totally different opportunities. Here's another angle for uncovering places to serve God. Circle how you would rather serve:

BY MYSELF	WITH FRIENDS
INSIDE THE CHURCH	OUTSIDE THE CHURCH
ONCE A MONTH	ONCE A WEEK
AS A LEADER	AS A PARTICIPANT
LEARNING A NEW SKILL	USING SOMETHING I DO WELL
AS PART OF AN ORGANIZED GROUP	ON MY OWN
WITH MY PEERS	WITH PEOPLE OLDER OR YOUNGER THAN ME
WITH THINGS OR TECHNOLOGY	WITH PEOPLE
FOCUSING ON EVANGELISM	FOCUSING ON DISCIPLESHIP
UP FRONT	IN THE BACKGROUND
AT SCHOOL	ANYWHERE BUT SCHOOL

Knowing your preferences might jog some ideas. Next, circle any of these ministry possibilities that sound interesting to you:

---

rehabbing house   sharing your faith with people you know   ministering in prisons

leading small group Bible studies   ministering through sports   dancing

cooking meals for shut-ins or the homeless   assisting unwed moms

teaching english to immigrants   leading Vacation Bible Schools   feeding the hungry

caring for children   cleaning and yard work for the elderly and single parents

helping with services at church—ushering, music, Scripture reading...anything!

counseling at Christian camps   performing with puppets   putting on plays

tutoring in basic skills like reading and math   painting

ministering in a nursing home clowning   visiting juvenile lock-ups

performing music outreaches   helping at an orphanage   counseling peers

evangelizing in public places   painting murals   distributing tracts

assisting senior citizens   taking prayer walks   encouraging new believers

stocking emergency food shelves and clothing closets   performing mime

counseling on phone-in hotlines   handing out Bibles   working at health clinics

---

Now look back at the items you circled. Pick a half dozen or so that feel most important to you and add them to your list above.

Are you starting to see some ways you could serve God right here, right now? If you've thought hard about your trip and worked through the lists yet still don't know where to serve, relax. That's fine! Plenty of people don't quickly dream up service ideas.

If you're still puzzled about where to plug in, start looking around. Is anyone you know doing something interesting? Start asking around. Do your youth leaders, Sunday school teacher, parents, or pastor have any ideas? Keep searching. God has a perfect place for you to practice.

WRAP IT UP WITH PRAYER

God, I want to keep serving you like I learned to serve on the trip. I want service to be part of my everyday life. Help me find the right place to practice.

CH.12

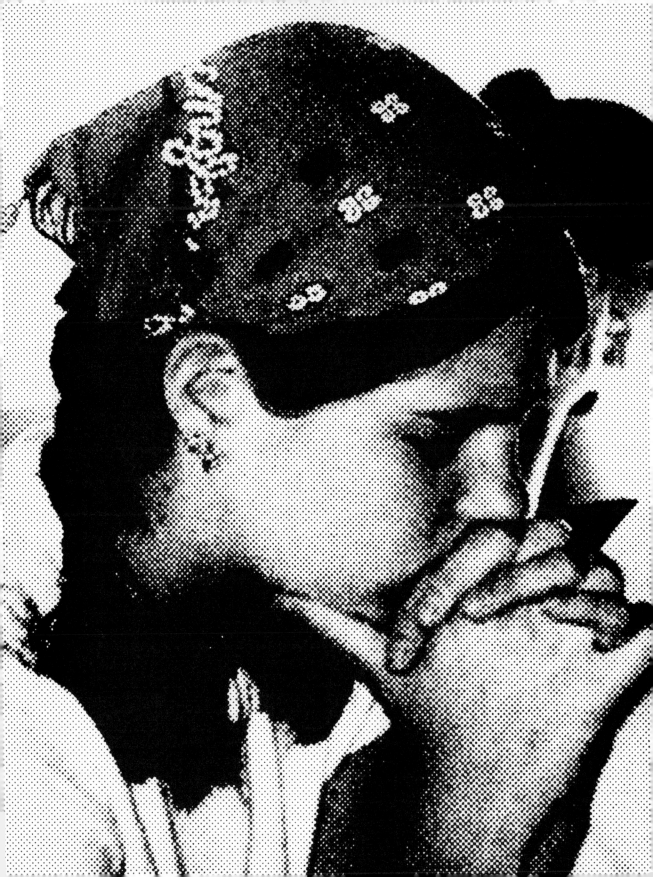

MAKING YOUR TRIP STICK

CH. 12

MAKING YOUR TRIP STICK

So you're home—or you're headed home soon. Maybe weeks have drifted by since your trip and you've readjusted to your at-home reality.

Here's a huge question: What about you has changed because you served on a mission trip?

_____

_____

_____

_____

Here's a related question—maybe the most important one in this book. First off, think big. Slingshot your brain far into your future—say, 10 years from now. Then answer this: How do you want your life to be different because you went on this mission trip?

_____

_____

_____

_____

Need some help? Think of the outrageous possibilities that could come about because of your hard work for God—and pick the one you prefer:

✝ The ultrastrong paint you slathered on an old house still hasn't peeled, and it holds the home together when a tornado levels the rest of the block.

✝ The little kids you taught still vividly recall all your stunning Bible stories—and one of them will grow up to be a world-shaking preacher.

✝ The people who helped pay for your trip are so impressed with your work that they offer you a job as your church's youth pastor.

✝ Your team leader writes you an earthshaking letter of recommendation—and the letter gets you a full ride at the college of your dreams.

✝ The cutest guy or girl on the team asks you out after the trip, and, to make a long story short, you get married and live happily ever after.

Hmmm... which seems best to you? Why?

_____

_____

_____

_____

_____

Those are all cool things that could happen—except for the superglue paint thing. Now consider one more possibility:

Everything you learned on your trip reshapes you permanently—and you make serving Christ an everyday part of your life.

That change tops all the others. It's the one that alters every bit of the rest of your life. But is that the kind of life-altering transformation you want? How do you like that option?

_____

_____

_____

The apostle Paul had a radical, life-long change after he met Jesus in the heavenly flash of light. When Paul in his old age wrote his second letter to Timothy, he wasn't playing shuffleboard and rocking away his final hours. He was in prison for preaching Christ. Paul's whole purpose in writing Timothy was to teach him how to hang on to everything Paul had taught him.

✝ "What you heard from me, keep as the pattern of sound teaching, with faith and love in Christ Jesus" (1:13). Paul wants Timothy to remember exactly what it means to believe right and cling tight to Christ.

✝ "Guard the good deposit that was entrusted to you" (1:14). Paul reminds Timothy never to lose what he's learned.

✝ "With the strength God gives you, be ready to suffer with me for the proclamation of the Good News." (NLT, 1:8). Paul says that serving God is worth any price.

At the end of your mission trip, you face the same challenge as Timothy of hanging on to what you've learned. You've tasted what it means to serve Christ. But how do you make that last?

Listen to Paul's secret—why he kept following God his whole life: "I know whom I have believed," he says, "and am convinced that he is able to guard what I have entrusted to him for that day" (1:12). Paul knew that whatever serving Christ cost him, it was worth it. God was safeguarding everything Paul had trusted to him.

Mission trips aren't just about doing good stuff. They aren't just about improving life on your planet. They're about staying connected to the God who sent you into the world in the first place. A single mission trip doesn't alter everything about you. But if it brought you closer to God and more in sync with his purposes, that's the change you never want to lose. You've grabbed more of God. Now hang on tight!

HANGING TIGHT TO GOD

Here's what your trip boils down to. You served so that others could glimpse Christ. So don't go and forget about what matters most. Of all the things you gained from your trip, sticking close to God is what you want to hang on to the most:

My three reasons why I want to stay close to God and keep serving him—with my whole heart, for my whole life

1. _____

2. _____

3. _____

Three things I commit to do to stick close to God

1. _____

2. _____

3. _____

WRAP IT UP WITH PRAYER

God, you are the one I serve. You make a life of serving you worth it. I want knowing you and making you known to be at the center of my life.

AUTOGRAPHS, ADDRESSES, AND E-MAIL

_____

_____

_____

_____

_____

_____

_____

_____

_____

_____

_____

_____

_____

_____

AUTOGRAPHS, ADDRESSES, AND E-MAIL
